THE BEST
DOGS
EVER

MASTIFFS ARE THE BEST!

Elaine Landau

🐾 LERNER PUBLICATIONS COMPANY · MINNEAPOLIS

To Karlan Sick

Lerner Publications Company
A division of Lerner Publishing Group, Inc.
241 First Avenue North
Minneapolis, MN 55401 U.S.A.

Website address: www.lernerbooks.com

Library of Congress Cataloging-in-Publication Data

Landau, Elaine.
     Mastiffs are the best! / by Elaine Landau.
        p. cm. — (The best dogs ever)
     Includes index.
     ISBN 978-0-7613-6083-4 (lib. bdg. : alk. paper)
     1. Mastiff—Juvenile literature. I. Title.
  SF429.M36L36 2011
  636.73—dc22   2010024222

Manufactured in the United States of America
1 — CG — 12/31/10

TABLE OF CONTENTS

CHAPTER ONE

WHAT A DOG!

Would you like to own a really big dog? How about one with a large, square head and a massive body? Just looking at this animal makes you think of strength and power. Is this wonderful woofer the dog of your dreams? If so, you've fallen for a mastiff.

Giant Canines

Mastiffs grow up to be very large. Below, an adult mastiff sits near a young mastiff.

Mastiffs are among the world's largest canines. Males stand at least 30 inches (76 centimeters) high at the shoulder. They can weigh 230 pounds (104 kilograms) or even more. That's about the weight of twenty-five house cats. Female mastiffs are a bit smaller.

NAME THAT DOG!

Every terrific dog should have a terrific name. Do any of these suit your mastiff?

Titan

THOR

Ursa   Diana

Hercules

Delilah   Jupiter

Venus

Sampson   SUMO

A mastiff's outer coat is straight and coarse. Its undercoat is thick and short. Mastiffs may be apricot, fawn (a shade of brown), or brindle (brown with black stripes). Their muzzles, ears, and noses are a darker color.

Grand and Good Natured

Mastiffs are much more than big and beautiful. They are also super pets. Don't let their size fool you. These dogs are gentle giants. Mastiffs are calm, easygoing, and loyal. These dogs want to feel like part of their human family. Many have risked their lives to protect the humans they love. Their owners think they have the best dogs ever.

A MASSIVE MASTIFF

One of the largest dogs on record was a mastiff. His name was Zorba (pictured above), and he came from Great Britain. When Zorba was eight years old in 1989, he weighed more than 343 pounds (156 kg). He stood 37 inches (94 cm) high at the shoulder. Zorba was also quite long. He was 8 feet 3 inches (2.5 meters) from his nose to the tip of his tail. He was one huge pooch!

CHAPTER TWO
MASTIFF HISTORY

Mastiffs are one of the oldest dog breeds. These dogs date back to ancient times. Drawings of them appear on the walls of Egyptian tombs.

The ancient Romans used mastiffs as war dogs. Roman soldiers dressed the dogs in armor. The soldiers led the dogs in attacks against the enemy.

Ancient artwork on the opposite page shows some mastiffs hunting. Below, a lion fights two dogs in a drawing from an 1825 book.

Later on, the English made mastiffs fight in peaceful times. They used the dogs in cruel sports to entertain the crowds. Mastiffs were pitted against bulls, bears, and even lions and tigers. Many mastiffs were hurt.

PATRIOTIC POOCH

During World War I (1914–1918), mastiffs served in the British army. These dogs pulled carts filled with weapons that the soldiers used in battle. The dogs' strength and bravery helped the troops.

People soon found a kinder use for mastiffs. People used the dogs to pull carts and carry heavy loads. They also used mastiffs as guard dogs. The mastiffs kept wolves away from livestock and protected their owners' homes.

A mastiff guards a carpenter's home.

THERAPY DOGS

Some mastiffs still work. They are trained therapy dogs. They visit people in hospitals and nursing homes. The mastiff's calm, easygoing nature makes it perfect for this work.

Mastiffs were great companions and workers, but most common people couldn't afford them. A mastiff was very costly to keep. These dogs eat as much as an adult human!

In Great Britain, butchers often owned mastiffs. Butchers had enough meat scraps to keep the dog well fed. That's why mastiffs were sometimes called the butcher's dog.

Crossing
the Sea

When did the first
mastiff come to the
United States? Some
say the dog sailed on
the *Mayflower* in 1620.
Did this huge pooch
really arrive with the
Pilgrims? No one
knows for sure.

The *Mayflower* may have
carried the first mastiff
to the United States.

But we do know that mastiffs became popular in the United States around the late 1800s. People often entered mastiffs in dog shows. Many people also used mastiffs as guard dogs. They made great family pets too.

A pet mastiff is captured in this artwork from the late 1800s.

This mastiff waits to be judged during the 2005 Westminster Kennel Club dog show in New York.

A Working Woofer

The American Kennel Club (AKC) groups dogs by breed. Breeds that have some things in common are grouped together. Some of the AKC's groups are the hound group, the toy group, and the sporting group.

Basset hounds are part of the hound group.

Yorkshire terriers are part of the toy group.

Springer spaniels, like this one, are in the sporting group.

The mastiff is in the working group. All the dogs in this group are large. They are also smart, strong, and hardworking.

Mastiffs have a strong build.

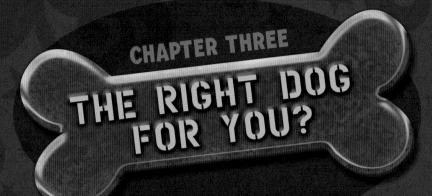

CHAPTER THREE

THE RIGHT DOG FOR YOU?

Mastiffs are marvelous. So shouldn't everybody have one? The answer is no. Although these dogs are great, they are not right for everyone. Read on to see if the mastiff is really your kind of dog.

Do You Have Space at Your Place?

Do you live in a very small apartment in a big city? If so, don't get a mastiff. These dogs take up lots of room. They do best in big houses with large, fenced-in yards. Did you hope to stretch out on your bed with your dog? Don't count on it. One of you is likely to end up on the floor, and it may be you.

Can't Go Far without the Right Car

Will your new dog fit in your car? An adult mastiff can't get into a two-door compact car. You'll need a van or a large sports utility vehicle for your furry friend. Even then, there might not be too much room for people once your canine cutie is on board.

HOW MUCH IS THAT DOGGIE?

Mastiffs are purebred dogs. Purebred puppies are pricey. It will also cost a lot to feed an adult mastiff. Can your family afford one? Be sure to discuss this with the adults who care for you.

A Slurpy Pal

There is no way around it: mastiffs drool and slobber. How do you feel about getting big, wet, sloppy kisses from a huge pooch? If you own one of these dogs, be sure to stock up on paper towels.

How do you feel about a dog that drools?

Quiet Nights

Do you plan on having your dog sleep in your room? If so, you'd better be a sound sleeper. Most mastiffs snore.

Could you sleep with a noisy dog?

A POOCH THAT NEEDS PEOPLE

Mastiffs are calm dogs, but they are not loners. They need to spend lots of time with their human family. Don't leave your mastiff alone for too long. You'll have one unhappy pooch.

Do you still think a mastiff is right for you? If so, you've made a great choice. You've picked a dog that's very loyal and loving. Mastiffs get along well with older people as well as young children. Your mastiff will make a fine family member.

CHAPTER FOUR

COMING HOME

The day you've waited for is finally here. It's better than your birthday and Christmas combined. This is the day you're getting your mastiff.

You've got your camera ready, but you'll want to have more than that. Not sure what you'll need to welcome Fido to your family? This basic list is a great place to start.

- collar
- leash
- tags (for identification)
- dog food
- food and water bowls
- crates (one for when your pet travels by car and one for it to rest in at home)
- treats (to be used in training)
- toys

Get Your Pet to a Vet

Don't waste any time in taking your dog to a veterinarian. That's a doctor who treats animals. They're called vets for short.

The vet will make sure your dog is healthy. Your new pet will also get the shots it needs. Take your dog back to the vet for regular checkups. And be sure to take your dog to the vet if it gets sick.

STICK TO DOG FOOD

Don't be tempted to give your dog table scraps. This can lead to an unhealthful weight gain. Pass on sharing your ice-cream cones with your pooch too.

Feeding Time

Give your dog good-quality dog food. Dogs need different foods at different stages of their lives. Ask your vet what food is best for your dog.

Your Best Buddy

Your dog will always be there for you. You can count on your mastiff to be a great friend. Make sure it can count on you too.

That means feeding and walking your dog even when you're tired or busy. It also means making your huge pooch feel like part of the family.

Be good to your dog, and you'll never regret it. You and your mastiff will make a terrific team.

START TRAINING EARLY

Training is very important with a supersized dog. A dog the size of a mastiff could easily knock over a child without meaning to. A well-behaved pet is a welcomed animal. You'll want people to like your dog—not fear it.

GLOSSARY

American Kennel Club (AKC): an organization that groups dogs by breed. The AKC also defines the characteristics of different breeds.

breed: a particular type of dog. Dogs of the same breed have the same body shape and general features.

brindle: brown with black stripes

canine: a dog, or having to do with dogs

coat: a dog's fur

fawn: a shade of brown

livestock: animals raised on farms and ranches

muzzle: a dog's nose, mouth, and jaws

purebred: a dog whose parents are of the same breed

therapy dog: a dog brought to nursing homes or hospitals to comfort patients

veterinarian: a doctor who treats animals. Veterinarians are called vets for short.

working group: a group of dogs that were bred to do different types of jobs, such as guarding property, carrying messages, or pulling sleds

FOR MORE INFORMATION

Books

Brecke, Nicole, and Patricia M. Stockland. *Dogs You Can Draw*. Minneapolis: Millbrook Press, 2010. In this book especially for dog lovers, Brecke and Stockland show how to draw many types of dogs.

Furstinger, Nancy. *Mastiffs*. Edina, MN: Abdo Publishing Company, 2006. This book provides interesting information for young readers who want to find out more about mastiffs.

Landau, Elaine. *Your Pet Dog*. Rev. ed. New York: Children's Press, 2007. This book is a good guide for young people on choosing and caring for a dog.

Markle, Sandra. *Animal Heroes: True Rescue Stories*. Minneapolis: Millbrook Press, 2009. See how the animals in these heartwarming true stories use their normal senses or special training to help people in need.

Websites

American Kennel Club

http://www.akc.org

Visit this website to find a complete listing of AKC-registered dog breeds, including the mastiff. The site also features fun printable activities for kids.

ASPCA Kids

http://www.aspca.org/aspcakids

Check out this website for helpful hints on caring for a dog and other pets.

LERNER *e* SOURCE™

Expand learning beyond the printed book. Download free, complementary educational resources for this book from our website, www.lernersource.com.

Index

Photo Acknowledgments

The images in this book are used with the permission of: © iStockphoto.com/Michael Balderas, p. 1; © iStockphoto.com/Julie Fisher and © iStockphoto.com/Tomasz Adamczyk (all backgrounds); © NaturePL/SuperStock, p. 4; © Cat Gwynn/Comet/CORBIS, p. 5 (left); © Mark Raycroft/Minden Pictures, p. 5 (right); © DreamPictures/Riser/Getty Images, p. 6 (top); © Jerry Shulman/SuperStock, pp. 6 (bottom), 10 (top), 12 (bottom), 14-15, 17 (bottom), 22 (right), 29 (top and middle); © Trinity Mirror/Mirrorpix/Alamy, p. 7; The Art Archive/British Museum/Gianni Dagli Orti, p. 8; The Stapleton Collection/The Bridgeman Art Library, p. 9; © Mary Evan Picture Library/The Image Works, p. 10 (bottom); © Erin Patrice O'Brien/Taxi/Getty Images, p. 11 (left); © iStockphoto.com/Erik Lam, p. 11 (right); © SuperStock/SuperStock, p. 12 (top); © Florilegius/Alamy, p. 13 (top); © Monika Graff/ The Image Works, p. 13 (bottom); © Jszg005/Dreamstime.com, p. 14 (bottom left); © Eric Isselée/ Dreamstime.com, p. 14 (bottom right); © Zach Holmes/Alamy, p. 15 (top); © Juergen Ritterbach/Vario Images GmbH & Co.KG/Alamy, p. 15 (bottom); © Casey Christie/The Bakersfield Californian/ZUMA Press, p. 16; © Tierfotoagentur/Alexa P./Alamy, p. 17 (top); © iStockphoto.com/Debi Bishop, p. 18; © Bryan Gladding/Dreamstime.com, p. 19 (top); AP Photo/Ajit Solanki, p. 19 (bottom); © Denise Hager, Catchlight Visual Services/Alamy, p. 20 (top); © Adogslifephoto/Dreamstime.com, p. 20 (bottom); © David Dalton/FLPA/Minden Pictures, p. 21; © Crystal Kirk/Dreamstime.com, p. 22 (left); © Tammy Mcallister/Dreamstime.com, p. 23 (top); © April Turner/Dreamstime.com, p. 23 (middle); © Geoffrey Whiting/Dreamstime.com, p. 23 (bottom left); iStockphoto.com/orix3, p. 23 (bottom right); © Michael Sofronski/The Image Works, p. 24; © Joy Fera/Dreamstime.com, p. 25 (top); © Jose Manuel Gelpi Diaz/Dreamstime.com, p. 25 (bottom); © South12th/Dreamstime.com, p. 26 (top); © Cheryl Ertelt/Visuals Unlimited, Inc., p. 26 (bottom); © Susan Law Cain/Dreamstime.com, p. 27; © Juniors Bildarchiv/F272/Alamy, p. 28 (top); © Dempster Dogs/Alamy, p. 28 (bottom); © Paul Bersebach/The Orange County Register/ZUMA Press, p. 29 (bottom).

Front Cover: © Howard Berman/Stone/Getty Images.
Back Cover: © Steve Wisbauer/Brand X Pictures/Getty Images.